JOY & BALANCE
Verses of The Old & New

CHRIS S. BOND

Copyright © 2022 by Chris S. Bond.
All rights reserved.

No part of this book may be reproduced in any form or by any electronic or mechanical means, including information storage and retrieval systems, without written permission from the author, except for the use of brief quotations in a book review. The events and conversations in this book have been set down to the best of the author's ability, although some names and details have been changed to protect the privacy of individuals.

Ebook ISBN: 979-8-9874406-3-6
Paperback ISBN: 979-8-9874406-4-3
Library of Congress Control Number: 2022922823

Cover & Layout Design: Sandra Schwartzman

Contents

Acknowledgments	v
Primo Poem	1
Blood Moon	2
Two Faces, One Clock	3
Bloody Ball Room	5
My Sweet Dear Child	7
Lavender	9
The Kings Tea Massacre	11
A Swan	13
Light	15
Th, thy?	17
Copper (Daisy)	21
Aloe	23
The Magician	25
The Monk Who Crossed the Sea	27
Lilith Is Dead, Hope Is Here	29
The Priest of Mourning And Purity	31
The Burning Palace	32
The Prayer Rest	33
A Hymn To Cherubim	34
The Red Of Cherubim	35
Why Do I Sin?	37
The Hymn, A Determined Holiness	39
Death	41
A Tale from Winter Death	43
Black Rain	51
Pripyat Is In Ash, Sleep, Sleep, Sleep	53
The Gas Mask	55
Demchenko	57

The Sacred Black Ash	59
Mystery Jazz	61
Can You Give Me My Whiskey?	70
Work: I Am A Slave	79
To Germany	88
The Red Bird, The Golden Dance	90
A Light Trumpet	92
A Cold Winter	94
The Mystical March	96
The Sweet Chocolate	97
The Tremendous Choir	99
The Tavern	101
The Golden Ring	103
The Rhinestones Of Gold	106
The Waltzing Cross	108
The Dawning Cry	109
The Ballroom at Night	111
The Astonished Waltz	113
Lavender And Vanilia	115
The Waltzing Stars	117
The Grave of Sixteen	119

Acknowledgments

I would like to thank my family, those who have stepped in along the way and especially Mr. Kevin Coble
and Cedric Fisher for opening doors for me.

We do not reach our destiny precisely on our own.

Those who say, *"good day,"*
"good morning,"
"hello and how are you?"
"you did a good job"
or *"you need to do some more work on this,"*
"you missed the mark,"
or *"this is just wrong,"*
"you need to go through that door or this door,"
"you can't do this or you will never be this," etc.

Hearing these words so much has given me those verbs and adverbs in my life at such a young age.
These experiences teach me that if you put your mind to it you can do anything, it is something to hold on to.

Joy & Balance

Primo Poem

I always wanted to see my daylight shine in glee.
But now I'm reduced to something
that I never wanted to be.
I became my own fear.
My own pain. My own past.
Living in something that I was reduced to.
I reduced it.
Me.
I did it.
I reduced my own worth.
My own life.

Blood Moon

I never knew that the sky could get so red.
While the moistness of my skin peels off.
The key unlocks to my bleeding heart.
While the victim's blood is on my hands.
While I paint in my sorrows.
The moon slowly cracks in its own time.
The rain is upside down.
This makes no sense.
I don't make sense. No one makes sense.
Except the one who makes the mistakes.
Can change history itself.

Two Faces, One Clock

Tick, Tock, Goes the clock, have you seen my mind?
Swirling around in the madness of the face of grief.
The ticking won't stop, have you seen my clock?
No sir, I have seen your faces in the mirror.
Back, and Forth, The Grief, The Astonished.
Leaned backed, Leaned forth.
Breathe my darling! Breathe!
I wish you not say that.
Do you hear a piano play?
Listen, Listen.
BANG! BANG! BANG! DING! DING! DING!
Have I killed your grief ?
My rain is here. This tragedy. My heart will beat!
To the rhythm! To The system!
Wait for it to fall. And I will stand tall.
And my grief will suck its thumb

and cry in its own flame of hell.
Down the well, with dreaming time, Chewing the lime,
waiting in the chime.
Two, Five, Six,
CHAOS! CHAOS! CHAOS! SYMPHONY!
SYMPHONY! SYMPHONY! DANCE! DANCE!
DANCE!
Breathe my darling! You are flying! You are an angel!
With your magnificent wings!
Soar higher, and higher.
Do you hear it? The orchestra? The waltz?
Hear it play.
Having it sway, This way, That way. The tune.
It feels the room of your royalness.
The Sword, SLASH! The Lighting, CRACKLE!
The Sun, BURN! TO ASH!.
No face. Only royal to the wings of the symphonies.
Orchestra, I hear you.
The Grief. The Astonished.
One face. Two face.
Tick..., Tick..., Tick..., Tick...,
Στον Απόλλωνα, σε ακούω.

Bloody Ball Room

As the blood drips down my face.
I can see my own thoughts.
The candle lights.
How they move from side to side.
The flame of beauty, how it looks, but how it feels.
The wax falling from grace.
The art of blood from paintings.
The smearing of it with its fallen waxes.
How smooth it is, coursing through my body.
Like a waltz, but with no luck.
But with its murderous tunes. The painting in the room.
How astonishing it is.

Oh, the blood!
I cry out.
As I waltz through the blood ballroom.
And as the towers fall.
The tune stops.
The blood waltz is gone.
Οι Θεοί, είναι ευχάριστοι

My Sweet Dear Child

She had the smoothest skin of silk.
He had the modest tunes of an instrument.
He loved her so much.
Her hair caught up in his face.
Her eyes glimmering in the twinkle.
His ways of her moves, swaying in motion.
The lies of her voice began.
The storms brewing.
The rain hitting his face.
Leaving him in the trace.
Walked away from him.
Oh, sweet dear child, don't cry.
I will take you away from these people.
Make you anew.
Make you stronger and the knowledge fill your mind,
Like a pot filling in water.

Forget the draught, my dear sweet child.
The dreams of his mind filled the air.
And so, did his faith. Sweet Child.
Orchestra calling him, the symphonies of his heart.
Brought forth a crown of pure gold.
And his piano, he was playing.
His sweet, sweet heart.
The crowd applauding, lavender, sweet, gone.
Στον Απόλλωνα, τον Δία, σας ευχαριστώ.

Lavender

I used to live in my dreams.
Wondering for hours and hours.
To see that time is fading away.
And my low self esteem as well.

So I scratch my skin and wait till I see the blood come out. And see the time of the hour go back to its normal state.
Waiting till the morning sun rises again.
But I don't see it.

All I see is rain and thunder. Does that bring me joy?
Or does it make it seem like I'm alone.
With just me and my thoughts.
Rambling off how the more time I see in myself.
The less I see in other people.

I face the mirror with those bleeding tears of mine.
Dripping down my face.
I call upon myself to bring the time with me.
At the last minute. The last hour.

The clock hits three. The lighting strikes me.
So I sit in a field of lavender. Watching the sky hit me.
With its blasphemous tune.

Now I lay here.
Bleeding out my dreadful sorrows.
So I can drown myself
under the darkness of my blood red skin.
So I wait for the orchestra to call me in.
At the last minute. The last hour.
The clock goes back to its normal state.

The Kings Tea Massacre

Long ago in a noble land, set a course of sand.
The king of rulers and strings sat atop on his
Throne of forbidden stands, pleased in his
Creation of lands.
Made himself a spot of tea,
Which forecasted the lakes and seas.
He took one sip, and the catastrophe came,
While the cup drowned in its ruins of the making
shame.
As the king once had the smile of gentle.
It began to rot in hatred with a scent of sentimental.
He raged on and on, throwing everyone out in demesne.
In a rowling hatred of his meins.
Crying on his throne over some spilled tea.
Walked and walked around
the circles of his own stupidity,

Crying out of his own inability.
Then the towers of his creation fell in a swing,
As the townsfolk fell in the whim of the bloody things.
Now, it's the king, once the rulers and the strings.
Now the forgotten wings.
His heart bleeding out of his chest, His body unrests.
Over the kingdom and fall.
Will still remain the same under all of them all.
As he still lays there.
Bleeding and crying all over the wall.
The realization of his own stupidity came to him
and ended with him a great fall.

A Swan

It is a heavy dew.
Without a sew.
When life gives these apples.
At this white chapel.
A great vastness of halls.
I walk through.
O, to be something in an endless time sake.
Thou is a ruin.
O, vita. O, vita.
Something so stubborn. O, something to vita.
At the pianos fall.
While this rose stalls.
A fire, flowing like water.
Fills this whole chapel.
Thou flowing through time.
Could be some kind of crime?

Without its soulful life.
A swan.
So elegant.
None could compare.
With no doubts than a hair.
A, such importance.
Such elegance.
O, vita. O, vita.
So importance, a swan, a vita.

Light

As I see it now, the sky glimmers in its twinkle.
Sitting by the ancient ruins of my home.
Lyre, Lyre, take me away with your strings.
Let it dazzle me in the sky of my home.
As I watch the mortals down below.
Sitting alone.
Playing this rhythmic tone.
In my home, Greece.
My aching body.
Laying, within its peace.
As I watch the olive greens grow.
My laurel for the poets, was no making shame.
A sign of beauty and knowledge of the great.
My father, lighting above.
His morals, and duties.
My mother, scorched in darkness.

Deceived, by my father.
Now, I pass on my light.
Through the trees.
Through the light.
Through the glimmering sun.
Throughout the minds of my prosperities.
Now, I lay here.
Playing my musical tone.
As the sky glimmers with delight.
As I hum and fly my hands through this gentle lyre.
In the ancient ruins of my home.
Απόλλων, σε ακούω.

Th, thy?

I see a room of green, parasols?
The lights flicker on, off
5th,
6th,
7th,
8th,
9th,
How can you let it go?
Parasites eating through the floor.
What's that on your shoe?
Blood, blood?
Blood screaming at me.
Show me your face grief.
The flame in his shoes, lighting fast.
Glitch, Glitch?
All I see is people.

Selling their soul for the fame,
The sex,
The drugs,
The th.
Don't say it.
Slowly going down a stream of blood.
The souls, th, th, th,
Don't say it fool.
Hand me a lighter with your lightning sides.
Smooth, relax, calming.
As I watch my heart, filled with diseases.
Of the toxic air of these fools.
Everyone making out 0n the 4th, 4th floor.
5th floor, smoke.
6th, worship?
7th, oh the holy grail of death.
Frames, frames, twice?
Not my problem.
Oh, sweet red.
Like strawberries, as they rot.
The crying, make it stop!
"I'll let my skin peel for your blood."
Says the man leaning to the sides.
With your lustful lies. Drunk with emotion.
Drunk with wine.
Prue blooded wine?
People dancing.

My work in flames.
The people in flames of deception.
Are you tired?
The dark soul of your eyes.
The love, Fake.
The devouring fears of devouring chance, luck?
Your silk black coat.
Why are you so cold?
I'll keep you warm.
The dancing of two shades of darkness.
We waltz in harmony of black spades.
The crows and ravens sitting in a coffee pot.
Sugar, spice, yes.
We are fighting in the life of our suffering.
Solving, reliving, receiving 12th, you lie.
13th, I cry.
14th, we smoke with our problems.
The blooded crown.
With the dark clouds of rain hitting us.
The crows following us.
The raven of our delight.
We reach, we grasp.
Feel the blood on our skins.
20th, hit me rain,
Let me cry in your arms.
25th, let me embrace your loyalty.
Spin, Spinning out of control!

The chaos, the confusion.
The recklessness of humanity.
4th, 4 steps of fear.
5th, the chiming of bells.
6th, The smoke of ravens' hair.
7th, one note, two note.
8th, The dead.
Start it over, start it over.
Echoes?
9th, th Beauty is terror.

Άδη, σ' ευχαριστώ.

Copper (Daisy)

How romantic!
The mist fills the air, how beautiful.
Spreading across the whole world.
To love.
All the copper will sing!
Dance and fling out towards the stars.
How beautiful…
But it will always come with a cost.
The greed of money.
Will spread like a disease.
And love will flee.
As the anges de cuivre watch.
Will find the greed and destroy it!
As the green paper falls down with burning ash.
The anges de cuivre will sing in a chorus tone.
Getting lower and Higher.

And greed will leave in no trace.
Towards a most subtle singing.
Of its Death.
As the sun gleams over the mystical planet.
It swings around the holy stars.
Breathing the life of love.
As it connects with all the mystical planets.
It stands still.
Love conquering the planet.

Aloe

Black, soft, and subtle.
Slow and the deepest darkest cold.
What could be ever asked from death himself ?
The falling, the falling.
Pure White then turns to Pure Black.
From a mind with an empty sack.
From a glimpse of a joyful sorrow.
What could be asked from the Onyx?
As the keys intertwine within each self.
Falling from the abandoned.
From my own shame.
For the key that which opens all doors to Nature.
For the flowers blooming in a way of pure delight.
The creation of all things.
Droughting the sorrow.
Droughting the light.

As rain hits my head for protection.

The earth has granted its full bows to all elements.

I see the light.

That no one can ever fight.

All the stars connect.

But no one can see with their disrespect.

It will always grow and flourish.

To find the days of the Prue.

Such sweet joyful sorrow I have.

As all humanity rests.

Nature grows in every breath.

The Magician

You seem distressed fellow.
Well, look no further!
Watch the cards fly!
And turn it into mellow!
Watch my hands
And all your manifestations understand.
It is all a trick of hand
But true creation at the palm of your hand.
Feel the scent!
Feel the breeze!
Could be and is the understanding.
I hold the instruments of your destiny.
But it is your will.
Pick up where you have left off.
And never ever stop the creation of your own destiny.
Feel the scent!

Feel the breeze!
Watch the birds chirp in harmony.
Now that is true nature, friend.
And is always your companion.
But do not be caught in the confusion!
Watch!
With a turn of a card to distract the confusion.
You have been fully transmuted!
To your imagination flies out of your hands
And cross your deep yellow sands.
Lavender with its strong scents within you.
Now that! Is the true art of the Magician.

The Monk Who Crossed the Sea

They crossed their desert way.
From soul to dismay.
How joyful rain fills upon the seas.
And scream out their joyful screams.
On the vast open shore.
Flowing through such deep water, I mourn.
And I stay here, forevermore.
Cold water, Cold Land.
In a storm filled with broken sand.
Carry out my dream.
Upon the vast seas.
Where they will come to me.
Through the storm, I mourn.
I have walked in the cold water of despair.
Yet, has not hit my feet with no care.
And light surrounds me with no pride.

Matariel, on my side.

I mourn through this heavy storm.

Everlasting glory comes through the heart.

But, wasted time?

No, never rot.

A dream to never be severed.

A joy to never be separated by lust.

To scream in pain.

To breathe in peace.

In this storm, I mourn.

With matariel, I am silent.

And peace has come to me so quietly.

As the boat rocks, back and forth.

I mourn in this rain.

With everlasting peace.

Lilith Is Dead, Hope Is Here

Majestic flowers grow in the garden.
To comfort the lost fellows.
With the brightest yellow colors.
And sin has washed away.
On the shore, ever blue nor red covered you.
And the black moon has vanished into
the nothingness of reality.
Thou the souls now carry stability and humility.
And I, carry the hope of the everlasting glory.
Thus, carries my story.
In the beginning, Lilith has swept us.
A drowning sea of everlasting despair.
And the soul was a slave to it.
In the end, flowed the light.
To break the endless cycle of the dead hope.
Smashing the despair from the lost souls, I cope.

And brings joy to the ode.

Woe to them!

Woe to them!

The fearful children that broke the despair.

Joyful angels scream beyond compare!

They have lost the will to despair!

They have gained the will to live!

A cry out.

A calling.

That they have asked for.

And found their way.

The angels carry them to the light.

The bright sensation.

To move forward.

And the angel of hope saith,

"And he shall reign forevermore!"

"For the lord, God Omnipotent reigneth!"

Hallelujah!

For I hope to wrap myself in this everlasting light.

And I am blessed for the joy of the world.

For it will spread like a wildfire.

For, The Hope is here!

For, Despair is Dead. Inside all of us.

The Priest of Mourning And Purity

I bring the mourning and the purity.
Under me, I hear you sinners.
I pray over you, always.
I scream to the heavens and say:
Holy, Holy, Holy, Lord God Almighty!
The sinners have been deceived by lust and greed.
They will change their ways.
O, Lord! It is in stone!
I cry to mourn.
I cry to purity.
The sinners of this world and mine.
Help us, o lord!
We shall see your true ever glory.
Holy, Holy, Holy, Lord God Almighty!

The Burning Palace

That palace.
That beautiful palace.
O, how so beautiful it is.
O, how it is now ash.
And that was my forever home.
As I see it burn to say its final goodbye.
I wave and say, Goodbye.
O, how beautiful that palace was.
And now, I cry for it.
Goodbye, sweet palace.
Till I see you again…
My forever memory.
My forever dream.
Goodbye my sweet, beautiful palace.
Goodbye…

The Prayer Rest

O, how I see the river side.
O, how I am covered in this beautiful light.
But darkness surrounds me.
O, how can this be?
I will cast the evil out of me!
I am the cherubim of this world.
I will light my incense and breathe in the deep holy.
The sage will knock on my door.
And I will cry out to the seraphim of seraphims.
I will tell the great things of this world.
Bless be! Bless be!
I sit here now with the trouble in me.
And ever graciously…

A Hymn To Cherubim

The golden red wings of pure wisdom.
I reach for the light of my God. And played ever gently in my word.
Come hither me Lord!
Come forth with thy wisdom.
To bring your everlasting cherubims.
The fine golden red of each wing is beyond compare.
And now I stare at the everlasting holy sun.
A flame which never burns out. Without a doubt! No doubt. The flowing wind I come to.
I mourn to be purified with truth.
A truth, A truth.
A flying everlasting truth…

The Red Of Cherubim

Sweet red of pure mystic flame.
Of Lord's wisdom, I claim.
A witness to wash away the sin.
In everlasting glory, it begins.
Watch as I fly with the wisdom!
To see the light in a mourning darkness.
Climbing the stairs of hope.
In order to cope with the mourning voice of Death.
And I weep and weep!
Until I cannot weep no more…
How I embrace in the lightness of my God!
And wisdom is bestowed upon me, like a crown.
Oh God! Oh Lord!
Oh Cherubim!
How I embrace in the light above.

Which darkness has fled below the surface of fire.
Oh, how I hear the sweet bells of wisdom
To my ears of glory, I thank thee, truly.
Praise thee for thy wisdom!
Praise thee for the hope has come.

Why Do I Sin?

Why do I sin?
Why do people sin?
A mourning family that I kin.
But, to and fro, where do I begin?
For something that is modern.
For something that is old.
Nor that which I am confused
A war that is corruptedly abused.
Casted light upon the table.
Darkness fell, the room is now stable.
No melody played the hope.
And people began to mope.
A rainy day that has stayed.
A solitude that has passed away.
Why do I sin?
No pleasure is forever.

And temptation has no endeavor.
For it only brings sorrow and pain.
And no hope there is to gain.
The repeating cycle of dread.
Will cease!
And now it is dead.
Why do we sin?
In holy light, I watch.
In a single line, a despairful march.
A light will reach them for hope.
And their souls will cope, cope, cope.
The drowning sea of despair approaches.
The calm waves of hope disposes.

The Hymn, A Determined Holiness

The Sun has screamed for centuries.
And waters have given you their gifts.
The Almighty God.
The most high!
Has given you hope!
And will pass on to generation and generation.
The sun, ever bright!
The singing angels, the everlasting glory.
Enlightened by the world!
The banging of drums, the rhythmic scene!
What can stop my god?
What can stop my god?!
With his Everlasting glory!
With his Everlasting glory!
What can stop my god!
The sea of dead.

Will dry up.
With everlasting glory!
God. My god!
The sun screams to hope.
And will reigneth forever!

Death

O, Death, I see you.
O, Death, I see you everywhere.
While I find my true self. You have always been there.
Right by my side, for the longest times.
While the rain pours.
While the sun shines on my face.
While the despair is frustrated.
You have always been there.
Like a guardian angel.
In the midst of the nights and days.
O, Death, Come.
While I fall to my despair.
While I rise up for hope.
It is truly an honour.
The life passes on, and I see you.
O! Death! Come!

In the light of days.
In the darkest of nights.
We will sit by the wintery pole and sing.
The whistles of the wind. The flowing of the breeze.
And, O Death, I see you.
Transforming the despair to hope, I thank you.
Walking with me forever on.
In all nights.
In all days.
We walk together in this black despair.
In the forever air.
And the sun shall shine upon us.
With hope in our souls, we are one.
O, Death, I thank you.
I thank you once more.
O Death, walk with me, forever on.

A Tale from Winter Death

Христос Спит

Eine Dunkle Nacht, Ein heller Tag Смерть, Я Жду Тебя

In the wintery cold, there is despair.
I can hardly breathe in this dreadful air.
After I leave my bloody footprints in the deep white snow. I will watch the black clouds roll in lumps of black muck.
There, I will reach my house in hopeful luck.
In there, warm, with luscious green air.
And the smell of cinnamon would dance without a care.
I, dread the senses out here.
No hope, no joy.
It is not even clear.
To see not one soul happy in this dreadful winter.

They will hide from the off-putting sounds of cinder.
No songs have been sung.
No lights have been turned on.
In that joyful house of mine.
Will be splendid! And my soul will be relieved.
This dreadful winter in its last despairful cry.
Will fall out and die.
On the wintery road.
Fallen.
There, I will reach my house in true joy.
And despair will reach out
its hand but slowly be destroyed.
When I walk through those doors and shut the door.
I will be forever pleased,
and sin will not hurt me no more.
The nice warm fireplace greeted me in light.
And smiled with delight.
No sin. No despair.
There will be rest for you.
In the harsh winds of drought.
So, we will close our eyes and rest in peace.

Blood, why blood?
Blood, the soothing?
The trapped mind.
And are we truly blind?
In the dark alley.

We cannot see.
Who can see? I can see.
See who? See he. He is the one.
An alpha? An omega?
Why do thy fingers hurt?
Why do I hurt?
In all questions.
Why do I hurt?!
The dark breaks the silence.
The people ask for guidance.
The light breaks the silence.
The people ask for guidance.
And the people have defiance.
And the people have no defiance.
From evil to good.
From which is evil?
From which is good?
And the people ask, why?
The Darkness speaks unto them:
"Which way is your way?
That is the way of the way?
So, ask, come forth.
In no life is simplicity.
Without drought and fear.
And why should pride guide you?
To a scorning sun that will melt your skin.
In agony, you cry.

So much false judgment falls upon you.
That you think you can
judge the innocent of their no crimes?
For which you will cry in pain, to hell with you!
And why will you feel the pleasure
to bring the innocent down from their innocence?
To bring your crushing demises to the joyful.
I say, that you fall out of place
and drown in a never-ending sea.
And why will you take away from the poor?
That have nothing except a raggedy body
and you wash it down with the shiniest of jewels?
I say, that death will follow you to the ends of the earth
and watch you waste away till your fire comes.
And why shall you manipulate
the innocent to do wrongfully?
For which they have no crime till you have used them.
I say, that in a quickness of your wrathful doing
will be swept up in the sky
and fall to the ground with a loud crash!
And why shall you manipulate the innocent to think
that they are no good because
you think you are no good?
A disease that you spread across the world.
I say, that your blood will spill
in the lake of your misdeeds.
And why shall will you eat the hand that feeds you?

That cares for your well-being?
That nurtures you back to health?
I say, that once you swell up with unhealthy habits.
You will burst and all will come out in blood.
And my final say to you,
why will you stay in your comfort
and say that you will put in efforts
in dreams and hopes?
To say that you will do something wonderful yet,
you lay back and watch the world burn.
I say, that you will fall in a deep haze
and unconsciously fall
back in and forth with what you have
done to yourself."

The Light speaks unto them:
"Which way is your way? That is the way of
the way?
So, ask, come forth. In no life is simplicity.
Without Hope and Joy.
I ask unto you, give yourself the humility
to bring forth your gifts
and share them with the world in good morals.
I ask unto you, give yourself respect to the other's wants
and needs and come forth to them with a proper
greeting in good morals.
I ask unto you, give yourself the charity to give back to

others in their time of need and you in your soul will forever be pleased in good morals.

I ask unto you, give yourself the patience to understand one another in the heart from their perspective of things in good morals.

I ask unto you,

give yourself the kindness for in people's mourning will need to be helped and comforted in good morals.

I ask unto you people,

Give yourself Temperance to the point of moderation of goodness in your heart.

I ask unto you my final people, give yourself the Diligence to fight for your dreams and hopes. Do not let them be manipulated or persuaded by the sins.

Amen."

And now people have found their own discipline and hope. As the world spins.

In this despairful, hopeful life.

We will see and watch with our eyes how the world turns and flourishes.

To pass on from generation to generation their good morals.

To follow the path of God.

To follow the light?

Yes, to follow the light.

O, sweet death.

I see you, I hear you.

O, sweet death. I will wait for you.
I will wait for you.
Once there is no more despair in this world.
No light. No despair.
A slowly calm rest.
But for now, I wait here.
And keep dreaming of new beginnings.
Which I hear stories from.
From its truest landscapes.
O! Sweet death!
I will wait for you.
I hear the laughter of children playing.
How sweet.
O, how so joyful!
O, joy. O, hope.
O, How beautiful this was.
But, O, sweet death!
I will wait for you.
In its truest tapestry.
How golden of lights.
How beautiful it looks.
The mirrors of my past are shattered into nothingness.
And all I see now is hope.
To bring into this despairful world.
A true life is knocking at my door
and I will answer with delight.
O, how we will see the light!

In its truest form.
O, every mourning.
O, every purity.
I see you. I hear you.
O, sweet death!
I will wait for you.

Black Rain

I stand alone in the forest. I am drowning in my sorest.
Over here, I hear the clouds of nigh.
The trees bleeding out, about to die.
As the black raven hides.
These trees forever die.
I stand in the midst of the black rain.
Over my house and city, it will reign.
As all the houses scream in pain.
I am slowly dying in this rain.
There is nothing left to give.
But, to be chained and outlive this dreadful land.
O, such despair!
It was planned!
Now, all I feel is the cold.
No story in this land can be told.
No mark, no scratch.

Only I am detached.
These cold blood red trees.
O, How they can see me weep.
And I offer myself to the black rain for peace.
O, such coldness!
I weep for release.
My soul is trapped in this forever tomb.
From which I can never bloom.
So I close the cold door.
And lay on this grassy dead floor.
I look up at this black rain.
Then reach out for cold, cold pain.
All I can do now is close my eyes.
And breathe in this cold, cold ice.
This is my calmness.
This is my home.
But I am forever alone.
Forever alone.

Pripyat Is In Ash, Sleep, Sleep, Sleep

The siren calls to me.
I hear the distant people running.
To the sun?
To freedom?
Should I stay or should I go?
The question is, where is everyone?
All I can hear now is the water dripping.
From pavement to pavement.
All I hear is nothing.
But that will give me something?
In the end?
Or in the future?
No one is here now.
I am the only one.
I see the stone of stones.
A great shine on these empty roads.

I heard two people died.

There is nothing I can do.

People are sick.

There is nothing I can do!

I run, I run far away from the disease.

The morse code on the walls.

I hear the distance beeps of what happened.

In fear, there is nothing.

I stand alone in this city.

Roaming in the distant valleys.

The eyes of illusion.

A haunting revelation?

Now, I only hear the beating of my heart.

It keeps getting darker.

No Hope, No Despair, No Fear.

I only hear the tapping of an old canvas.

From which there is beauty in the air.

Keep me safe life!

There is nothing more here.

The Gas Mask

The work is hard.
The black raven can send my regards.
The smell of fresh pine and sage.
On the outside, the world is just phage.
No similar to any other.
But I wish to see my brother.
In other times.
In other worlds.
How time just swirls and swirls.
The work is hard.
The black raven can send my regards.
On the outside world, Is forever grey and blue.
In these meadows, I get a good view.
The Black Raven can send my regards.
The work is hard!
The outside world is forever turning.

And I am forever seeing.
I have gone mad.
The work is hard!
The Black Raven can send my regards!
My work is hard.
My Black Raven can send my regards…
These fertile soils grow.
But my low is slow.
And forever decaying.
The work is hard, I'm staying.
The Black Raven can send my regards, I'm praying.
I work and work…
I work and work…
The Black Raven… The Black Raven…

Demchenko

Who are you?
Who am I?
Do you understand me?
Do I understand you?
I wish you understand.
Understand why.
Why of the understanding.
Do you like to dance?
Do I like to dance?
Do you understand?
Do I understand?
Your homeland.
My homeland.
How sweet.
How delightful.
In all tones, do you understand?

O, how I missed you!
O, how I missed our homeland!
And now we walk on an unknown land.
And, O, how!
This unknown land.
Is now a part of me.
Deep inside the unknown of a tree.
A mysterious sap.
That you drink from like a tap.
Who are you?
Who am I?
I am you.
I am I.
How mysterious!
How strange to ask a question!
Demchenko.
Demchenko is my name.
Who am I?
I am… I

The Sacred Black Ash

O, my heart throbs out.
To see those black clouds.
O, sweet gasoline.
Come to me.
Forever free, forever free!
O, protect me with this smell of pine.
So, for this, I will not die.
I will not die!
I read these sacred ashes.
Of quick, those angels, dashes.
O, sacred ashes.
The smell of your dullness.
A pure spark of willingness.
My mind is forever free in the smells of pine.
So, I will not die!
So, I will not die.

I am forever walking towards your gracious ashes.
So, I can smell the sweet dullness of angelic dashes.
O, sweet sacred ashes!
O, sweet sacred ashes!
The blood from trees.
A sacrifice to the ends of meat.
How sweet the sacred, sacred ashes!
O, sweetness. O, brightness.
I feel the burning sensation of judgment.
To make me a sacrifice of your holy judgment!
O! How it delightfully burns!
And now it is the tree's turn.
O, sacred ashes.
The beautiful sacred black ashes.
The angelic dashes!
I bleed with the delightful flow.
O, my skin gives me a sweet glow.
Now, I rest eternally, ever so slowly…

Mystery Jazz

A howling cry.
For sure that I might die.
But, I will keep smoking.
And drinking my whiskey.
It is so bold. So strong.
Yet, So dark and cold.
It is grey in my homeland.
And my blues are forever crying.
On this dark, cold night.
On this black abyss, my mother was right.
The world is gone and shameful,
And I pity the ones in a sorrowful dose.
I can't say anything though,
I can't compose.
In this black-and-grey world.
There is nothing I can do,

yet drink my sorrows away.
The ones that say I am wrong.
But they are not strong and forever wrong.
I speak with my blues.
In confession:
I speak to them with honesty.
And they speak to me with modesty.
In a crazy world like this.
Is a spinning disc.
A forever merry-go-round.
In shades of navy blue.
And my smoke will never cure you.
I sit outside, in droughtful pain.
Waiting for them to see me again.
It could get me killed, yes.
But it is strong as this whiskey!
And there is quiet screams in everyone's head.
Even myself, my soul is filled with dread.
If I ever could walk in the sun again.
And forever be young again.
That could be my pleasure.
But, it has all died out.
And forever rotting in my soulless cell.
If I ever could walk again.
If I ever could be free again.
That would be my pleasure.
But, there is no doubt.

That it is gone, from my homeland.
It is all a chamber with chains.
And everyone has the blues.
It could mean that I'm out of tune.
So is everyone here.
All rotting in a soulless cell.
No vessel.
Just strings attached to us.
And we are, forever dying. Could there be hope?
For me?
For us?
No.
It is not possible now.
It is only a myth with a tragic tale.
But, for now, I drink my whiskey.
On the side porch of this vast smokey land.
Yet, My heart is soulless.
And is broken in tune.
Like, the sad, sad, blues.
Cry if you want.
It is already done.
A future that is so gloomy.
But I have lived in one.
Could mean a meaning.
But without one?
There is no one.
And it is rotting.

Forever rotting inside, each and every soul.

All I can do is listen to my blues

and smoke this night away.

On my favorite porch.

A sad lonely porch.

A forever doomed porch.

But, I am that porch.

Why do you think I'm good?

There is nothing good.

My soul is forever chained.

And, forever gone.

There used to be good.

In this world.

But,

All I see is the forever chains of people.

The violence…

The violence…

The violence…

In a city road like this.

It is only agony in pain.

The pain in agony.

The illusion of this world.

A "Perfect World" In their eyes.

All of us die in this "Perfect World" of theirs.

A feather plucked from the beautiful raven.

My raven…

My raven…

My raven…
I curse you new world! You have ruined us!
You have ruined me!
And, for what?
To live high?
In your perfect sky?!
While I rot?
While we rot?
In the black soil that you made.
A deep, dark shame.
It is all an illusion.
For your construction.
To build yourself higher and higher.
Till you see nothing more on the ground.
You do not care.
We only care for ourselves now.
And, no.
I will not pity you.
For you have brought shame and agony across this land!
My fatherland! My homeland!
You crush the hopes of children.
Now they are slaves.
For your lustful pleasure.
The children have the blues.
We all, have the sad, sad, blues.
You broke the hopeful piano.
And burned its beautiful scores.

Now that you have,
What pleasure do you have?
For destroying the world?
What are you?
A monster, yes.
A monster indeed.
There is so much crying.
There is so much shouting.
For you, have made this.
Will it change?
No guarantee.
No guarantee…
But, I watch the illusion be trapped in minds.
Sucking the hope of beautiful people.
Just break. In insanity?
Or in blues?
There is no clue.
And no sap of delightful dew.
It is a black, grey, and navy.
No more, No less,
No forever rest.
But in pain.
In agony.
As deep blues sing.
I got the blues!
Yes, Indeed.
Till the morning.

Till the darkest night.
I wake from this illusion.
But what can you do?
Keep hoping.
You say?
Keeping dreaming.
You say?
Keep believing.
Yet, You say:
In all modesty. In all honesty.
Keep hoping, I say.
But,
People keep sleeping.
You say?
People keep dying.
You say?
People keep destroying.
Yet, In all honesty.
In all modesty.
Keep believing, you say.
You have the dream.
You have the gift.
You have the light, I say.
In chains, were, and are broken.
Half awake. Half asleep.
I drink my whiskey.
And keep dreaming on the blues

The forever blues.
It is all dark in my fatherland.
It is all light in my homeland.
Can you keep on dreaming?
Can you keep on believing?
"Can you keep on obeying?"
They say: with no modesty.
No honesty.
It is an illusion.
Forever an illusion.
No more crying. No more dreaming.
No more believing.
And, I still sit on this porch, drinking my whiskey.
Watching this "Perfect World" go by.
In a flash of night to day.
There is still forever weeping.
Inside my soul.
From where I broke from the illusion.
It is weeping in my heart.
Under this porch, There are bodies, Who built this place,
Forever crying, Forever yearning.
And, Yet,
My whiskey is gone.
And my sorrows are gone.
But, Yet,
Where is my joy?
Go find it.

In this deep, illusionary void.
What can you do? Go find that joy.
In humble singing.
No more smoking.
No more drinking.
I pluck from my black raven.
And color it with blood.
The blood of the sweet blues.
And forever on with the sweet tunes.
To change the way, how can that be?
To change, I guarantee.
Unto you, Unto me,
Yet, To change,
is my forever yearning.

Can You Give Me My Whiskey?

They done did me wrong.
Yes, indeed.
The impoverishment of life hits me with impact.
And I have to hate the people around me.
Even though, I question it.
With the sentimental of low life.
And it even scares me.
That people hurt people like this.
In this day and age of this new world.
Why?
Why do you do that?
You want me to have the blues?
You want me to cry?
I won't let you have my mind.
So you can go read your own notes.
Watch and dose off.

CAN YOU GIVE ME MY WHISKEY?

And don't pay attention to me.
Let me be in peace.
For goodness sake!
Let the man cry and weep on his own time.
For you have caused this scene.
For you think you are the judge of his life?
You can fly somewhere else!
Bye Bye Now!
Good riddance.
Can you give me my whiskey?
Since you won't have to be so frisky.
They want us to be their slaves.
For their good will.
I think not!
You can dot that with morse code with me!
I find this irritating.
Do you?
I hope you do.
They drink up my hopes and put me in chains.
Good Riddance!
I say?
What is their plan?
To be holy?
To be good?
If you were good.
You treat me with good will and respect!
Good Riddance!

I say!
They have no hope.
But hope for themselves.
They care about their feelings.
Their actions.
How dirty can you truly be?
I cry out!
In agony!
How long will humanity be like this?
In agony!
And it truly gives me the blues… I ask truly.
How will this be read?
In my whiskey is true blues.
From these crimes.
For they are the judgers of judges.
On themselves. And onto others.
It will make them cry?
Do you want that, boy?
For them to cry in this impoverished world?
We die because of this! In these painful ways.
By your actions, you done did me dirty.
Will you help those people?
Or are you selfless enough to turn the other cheek.
And watch them die, die, die…
My whiskey is in the blues, I tell you.
All in the blues from this impoverished world.
To the prohibition of myself.

CAN YOU GIVE ME MY WHISKEY?

It will cry from the inside.
And I will cry along with it.
It is a stone-cold world, I tell you.
How you judge them like a devil with no good excuse.
From down here, in Mississippi.
It is just like my whiskey.
The strong boldness for yourself.
But, it could be set ablaze from your own prideful manner.
To not help.
To not care.
Nobody cares!
It is only for themselves!
And they dash away.
And they fly away.
Like it isn't their fault.
They cry to their momma.
They cry to someone who thinks they will take their side.
Please! Bye Bye!
Good Riddance.
They think they're special on high statues.
In high places.
And they call me a pain?
Oh, please! Goodbye!
Good Riddance!
I rather sit here with my whiskey.

I do not care.

I do not care for you.

Call me whatever you want.

I do not care.

Goodbye and see you never!

But in the quietest anger.

In the quietest impoverishment.

To be a slave to their deeds.

Hope is called.

The messenger.

Will seek you out.

And play you the humble sweet tune jazz.

Oh, that sweet saxophone!

I can hear its calling.

And I'm listening.

And I'm standing.

To find its true tune.

To fight in this impoverished world!

With me and the messenger, finding true hope.

Oh, my friend.

It spreads like a wildfire.

To give those joys is true charity.

With my half-empty whiskey.

Sing me a tune, messenger!

So we can find the right people in good tune.

Oh, messenger.

Sing me that true tune!

With all quiet blues.
It is all in the world's gain.
To bring the messengers hope to you.
For you are the pain.
You are in the agony.
But, we'll sing and dance with this new groove.
Watch the messenger dance.
In his dancing prance!
Watch us bring you hope.
You need it.
We all need it.
We few,
Follow in the messenger's tune.
Oh, bring the light!
My messenger.
Our messenger.
That curse in us is gone.
And we follow our own steps.
Our guiding spirit: the messenger.
We say to him:
"Bring us out of the hatred and pain!"
Even though we ought to do it for others.
But, it is our selfishness and greediness that is blocking it.
And true pain will come with it.
Let us few,
Walk in the messenger's steps.

While we still can!
I might be the blues of a drunken man but I speak the truth!
We dance in our drunken ways.
But do we care?
Who knows!
It is the drunken foolishness.
But it is our transformation at the end.
Follow the Hope!
It is the trumpet's understanding.
The singer's composition.
For the Band!
Which is which in this world?
We follow the chosen paths.
Of hope.
They told me in my drunken haziness.
I am following that same light today, boy.
It follows you.
It follows us.
For understanding.
For our emotion.
But,
In every way.
We few,
We'll give the hope to people.
In the messenger's voice.
But,

For these lost souls.
Give them charity.
Because,
They have been lost in fornites.
On end with no ending.
Oh, and they plead for them to breathe.
From under the Prideful sun.
But, Listen hear, boy.
Can you give me my whiskey?
For we will still have the blues for now.
But,
There will be a time where we are equal.
And have charity for one another.
And have light for one another.
For one another, I say,
It will give us hope in no pride.
No greed.
It is a troubled time,
Indeed.
But in the darkest troubles.
When It gives into the darkness.
My heart.
Our hearts.
Unite. As one.
It will spread like a wildfire, boy.
It will find us.
And follow us.

Telling our stories.
Forever on into nothingness.
With no more tunes.
Just the blank white stare.
It lets me feel at ease.
Riding along this vast blue wave.
And we morally crave.
But, it is human.
We both work in
The Logical and The Emotional.
How far we can sing in our deep, sad blues.
Only time will tell, my friend.
But, I say,
My friend,
The boy with the blues,
Can you give me my whiskey?

Work: I Am A Slave

For this is: war.
It is a life that has enslaved me.
Drought me.
Deceived me.
It will bleed out.
In many messes.
It ruined me.
It killed me.
Even though,
I still stand tall in this despairful world.
Who has the blues?
I do, I do,
Let the slow rhythm take me away from here.
Far, Far, Away.
The world is dying in all words.
In all worlds.

In all,
It has deceived me.
Yet, Yet,
I stand tall through it all.
But, I am a slave.
To work through these messes.
In all creation.
It has enslaved me.
From all wrong.
From all right.
From all that was in the end.
I stand tall.
But,
To be slaved?
I will never be.
I need to stand tall.
Follow that motto.
In all works.
In all tapestries.
In all blues.
I want to stand tall.
Yet, I am.
Yet,
I will.
Let me cry out to it.
For peace.
For joy.

For happiness.
In this despairful world.
My sweet violin plays.
In a broken orchestra.
From candle lights aflame.
It is all a forgetful shame.
Let it cry out,
Once more,
For Peace.
For Joy.
For Happiness.
All around.
The blues stand tall with crying nor all.
Let it fall.
Let it rain.
Once again.
Let it rain.
Let it fall.
We all should stand tall.
For goodness sake.
Stand tall!
With confidence.
With dignity.
With diligence.
Time is of my soul.
Work after work.
Day after day.

Night after night.
It is all work.
Time.
Find me.
Look inside of me.
Don't you see that I have the blues?
Let me cry.
Let me cry.
Let me work.
Let me die.
There is no other choice, time.
I work and work.
Day and night.
I am a slave to it.
With wisdom.
With life.
With no guarantee.
It is all dark in my vision.
But to you. Have light.
Give the light.
Do not drought on the inside.
My friend.
Do not drought on the inside.
Let your heart grasp the temptation of confidence.
To break a cycle of hate and torment.
While for me.
I walk alone.

In this dystopian town.
It could.
It can be fixed.
With your light.
Your hope.
Enjoy the freedom while you still can.
While it is done.
Time,
Take me,
To the clouds of an unreached land.
Let it drive me.
Let it fly.
Like the red birds in the sky.
Fly high, Fly high.
O, time.
It is coming weary.
I feel the awful drought of tears.
And the rain washes it away.
Let me cry.
Let me cry, time.
It is your essence that I work.
Day in,
Day out,
Though the spirit does not care for you.
I do.
It is your essence of my completion.
Let it fly.

With me.

In the melancholy of this world.

Black and white.

White and black.

Let it rain!

Let it pour!

It is all I ask of you.

Let it rain,

Let it pour.

To wash my tears away.

I have the case of the blues.

Let me cry with you, rain.

Time will watch us. In every second.

In every hour.

Let the rain inside of me fall in. And my hole will slowly cave in.

O, I work.

Day and night. Every weekend. Of every month. Of every hour.

It drains the soul out of me.

Today, We stand tall.

It all goes in a stage fall.

For the blues and I.

Have gotten stronger.

Of every hour,

Of every month,

Of every day.

O, blues, let it sink in.

Into the vast black sea.

Where it drowns it leads up to hope.

In a crashing blow.

With the sea,

It drowns me.

But today,

I stand tall.

Through it all.

Let it rain, time.

Let go of time, rain.

Let it all balance out.

With more joy. With more blues.

Inside of me.

On a joyful sorrow day.

I work and work and work.

Day in, Day out, I stand.

Today, We stand.

In the midst of a great storm.

Let it turn me in.

Let it turn me out.

Let me have joy.

Let me have joy.

In all tapestries.

It will lead to the greatest joy.

Let it rain.

Let it fall.

Let me give it to art.
And paint it with the shades of gray.
With shades of navy blue.
In my darkest corners of black.
Let the time in.
Let the rain in.
For no one is perfect.
O, I am a slave! For wisdom.
For diligence.
For freedom.
Let it all run into me with great force!
For it is truly beautiful.
In all creation.
It is truly beautiful.
Do not let my ink dry.
We are still able to write these letters.
You and I.
To Time.
To Rain.
To All.
It is all in tapestry.
For we have the hope.
The joy.
The happiness.
To achieve.
I guarantee.
I guarantee.

I break these chains.

And I will no longer be a slave.

To myself.

To break in my desperate freedom.

I see clearly.

I see now.

I see…

To Germany

Wave that new flag, in hand!
To my sweet fatherland.
I thank you for opening my eyes.
I shed my tears and cry.
I follow every step.
In joy, my fatherland!
We follow our modest land.
I watch and gaze.
There is despair everywhere.
But my fatherland, find the joy.
Find the hope again.
O, my sweet fatherland!
I can forever stand.
Watch and gaze.
For my sweet fatherland.
There will be joy in the most sorrow hours.

In my fatherland.
Follow your joy with your unity.
Keep your chin high, my fatherland.
Watch and gaze with that joyful flag.
I wave that flag with courage and dignity.
For freedom, I watch.
For freedom!
My fatherland!
We are in unity with that flag waving.
For my fatherland!
I thank you.
In the coldest winter.
I thank you, my sweet fatherland.
Grias Godd!

The Red Bird, The Golden Dance

The sweet melody.
Forever turning.
In a great dance.
It puts me in a trance.
In a low tune.
A sweet, subtle smell of perfume.
I dance with the golden trance.
Let it take me away.
In all tapestry!
Take me away and let the cup sway.
I see the red bird.
On the birch tree.
I stare and wonder, what if it is me?
Slowly swaying with the red bird.
And my blood would speak without a word.
I dance the night away.

With the sweet red tune,
I forever sway.
Could it mean my blood is forever turning?
I am swaying.
I am swaying.
And the red bird is forever looking.

A Light Trumpet

The angels march in order.
They sing with each other.
To dance.
To fly.
In freedom, they dance away.
"No more cares today!"
They say A sweet drastic tune.
But the angels forever roam in tune.
Singing the carols.
Singing the gospel.
The lovely tune that they sing is delightful.
With confidence and diligence, it is impactful.
How they sing!
With trumpets galore.
With flutes fluttering around.

With the bassoons in sweet harmony.
With the dance of care and free!

A Cold Winter

The trumpets call.
The carol bells sing in aw.
Like from fire to snow.
It repeats its goals.
A cold winter.
With nothing more.
Then snow galore!
It turns to fire.
It turns to snow.
A joyful show at the ballroom.
Where I see ballets in harmonic tune.
There is something calling the snow.
And I see no more shows.
It is gone.
Nowhere to be seen.
Like fire.

A COLD WINTER

Like snow.
I see the candlelights light aflame.
In the brisk, cold snow.
Where it warms in a fiery bellow.
A fire.
A snow.
Dance away in the bosom of the world.
With no gloom.

The Mystical March

The charm.
The glory.
We walk strong in our faith!
And the diners dine.
And the dancers dance.
And we march, march, march!
To the slow roaring tune.
We march, march, march!
And our circus begins with scratch.
And we go, tap, tap, tap!
For our family.
For our friends.
And we, march, march, march…

The Sweet Chocolate

The fair aroma. Of sweet chocolate.
Dazzling in the new day bew.
It was so sweet!
It was so strong!
The aroma comforts me.
In all the tapestry.
It makes me dance.
And I will forever do.
O, the sweetness.
O, the joyfulness.
It brings me.
It could hold on tight.
And it would know that I'm right.
It is so fair. It is so sweet.
It is the ever lasting kiss.
O, so fair!

So sweet…
We are one in harmony.
We dance in rhythmic beats.
A call to us, we hear.
From a far. It could be me.
It could be us.
But we dance the night away.
In all tapestry!
I swollemly say:
"The dance we write, is sweet with delight."

The Tremendous Choir

How they sing.
How they sting.
How they guide us.
How they follow us.
With a loud bang!
It is all low and loud.
It is all outstanding and proud.
We see each other cry.
No more, no less it is on the inside.
With a bang!
And the bells ding!
The choir takes head.
With the blasting orchestra following.
And they sing!
And they sting!

How they guide us along the trails.
How we follow in moving tales.
It is all beautiful.
And the most mystical scales.

The Tavern

In the tavern.
The men drink.
In the joyful bosom.
They drink and drink.
Till they get drunk!
It is their time to shine!
They clap their drinks and dance away.
They dance their night away.
And sing joyful tears.
About their mothers fears.
They clap.
They sing.
With joy in their cups.

Hanging over with joyful slumps.
On those dark, red sofas.
In their joyful bosom.
They drink.
With joy and compassion.
While they sleep in cold stimulation.

The Golden Ring

The golden ring. However, can it be? The golden ring.
In all of its tapestry!
The Golden Ring.
With all of its glories!
In all tapestry.
The Golden Ring.
The Golden Ring However, can it be?
The Golden Ring.
In all of its tapestry!
The Golden Ring.
I fly on its wings!
In all golden tapestry.
In the snow.
In sweet snow.
In the cold.
In sweet cold.

I feel the dying cold.

In the fire.

In sweet fire.

In the hot.

In sweet hot.

I feel the dying warm fire.

In the snow, I crash!

In the fire, I burn!

In all of its tapestries.

The golden ring.

In all of its tapestries!

The golden ring!

I see my fate in heavy rain.

The Golden Ring.

However could this be?

The Golden Ring.

I see the bloody thing!

The Golden Ring.

How could this ever happen to me!

In all the bloodiest things.

I see blood.

I see cold.

I see fire.

I see blood.

I see no one.

I see only one.

I see blood.

THE GOLDEN RING

I see fire.
I see the warm hands.
I see, in all tapestry.
The Golden Ring.
The fire is burning.
The cold is melting.
The fire burns me.
The cold runs away, hiding.
I hear the loud crash!
In fiery tapestry!
I hear the loud boom!
With no trance!
My Golden Ring.
The cold crashed!
It is gone.
The cold crashed.
It is well done.
The sweet, Golden Ring.
The Golden Ring.
I am bleeding from harmony.
The Golden Ring.
I spill my blood in me.
The Golden Ring.
I curse you inside of me!
In all the great bloody tapestries.

The Rhinestones Of Gold

In the sky, O, glamorous.
The sky sings from every corner.
In my eyes it is just one corner.
But in the sky's eyes it is every corner.
Upon pavement after pavement.
Filled with luscious gold.
It has a heart for no one can tell.
The chimes of bells with no swells.
But dashing on the snowy rails.
It is all quiet here.
It is all loud here.
With scents of beer.
Drinking upon every hour,
every corner.
It Could mean something to you.
Or what is inside of you is true.

In my eyes it is glamorous.
In the sky's eyes it is wonderfully true.
A final stage where it comes to my longing.
And so far.
The sky and me are rhyming, dreaming, believing.

The Waltzing Cross

In the flaming cold night.
I see the shining star of light.
For it waltzes with people.
There is nothing like this light.
The cold flaming image of the cross burns inside.
With hope along the side.
In the dark cold winter it rises.
With the cross at hand
and they pop up with more surprises.
The Waltzing Cross.
In my dreams forever telling me.
What is and isn't on the scales of justice.
It balances the sways and the cold heart of mine.

The Dawning Cry

I see the blood.
The blood, I see.
I lay there, weeping unimaginably.
I cry, I cry.
And my heart is slowly dying.
I lost it all ago.
To think that was ages ago.
I cry, I weep for you.
Finding nowhere to go.
And my blood will run away because I have no control.
I weep, I cry for you.
But that was ages ago.
The blood, I see.
Let me weep.
Let me cry.
I want to slowly die…

My crime.

My punishment.

How can this be?

With no waltz dancing for me?

O, the pain.

O, there is no gain.

I have fallen out of frame.

On the side where I bleed,

I am ashamed.

So let me weep.

Let me cry.

I am always dying on the inside.

Even the moon can't cry for me.

Even the sun can't cry for me.

My waltz is broken and gone.

Let me bleed out with my broken soul

and my forever dawning wisdom.

The Ballroom at Night

It is forever quiet.
With the low painful tune.
For, who knows, it could be you.
Taken up from the night.
It is blasphemous!
The blasphemous tune.
Of sweet sorrow and pain.
There is no hope to gain.
In this cold night.
It will freeze over the land.
How far can I stand?
This is night.
Where we sing with not a blight in sight.
The quiet creeps in with flashing cold.
Almost on a catastrophe night.
It hits us with the blasphemous tune!

Once more, forever in swing.
It is a cold night.
Forever draughting in crying nights.
It could scream.
It could bleed.
But the quiet waltzes with us.
So silent.
So calm.
In the coldest hours.
In the highest towers.
In the lowest taverns.
It comes with calmness.
A pleasure to have on these coldest hours.

The Astonished Waltz

It is all quiet here.
On this frosty night.
I stand under the half moons twilight.
I see those same stars over there.
To the northwest.
How astonishing it is.
With a blowing windcrest of air.
How astonishing it is.
The clouds roll in.
For the performance I cry in.
It dances almost freely.
In that same way, make me steady.
On those nights.
Where I see the twilight sky.
In perfect mystical harmony.
Yes, what a mystical army.

Of instruments galore.
It stands right under the moon's core.
How astonishing.
How pure.
With mystical air onto you.
Onto me within its truest tapestry.
I thank thee.

Полумесяц

Lavender And Vanilia

Sweet, sweeter.
How can that be?
A flow of pure water, I see.
The color of shade, in pure blue seas.
The quick dash of air.
How can that be?
O, sweet aroma.
Follow me everywhere around.
In the quickest of air.
In the pure water of delightful air.
And my sweet air said to me:
"I dance freely, with no care!
No troubles!
Blessed in you,
your fiery sun,
your twilight moon"

The quickest air.

Follow me with no cares!

O, sweet aroma.

Follow me everywhere around.

A passion from the air's eyes glimmers under the twilights.

Of stars,

Of passions,

Of pure bliss.

And my fair aroma said to me:

"I care in bliss, A sweet tender care!

Your passion, your chastity,

Blessed in you, your twilight moon, your fiery sun"

Speak to me with flow and follow me wherever I go.

Because of this dark cold snow.

It will freeze the tapestries.

Inside of me, carefree, sweet aroma in me.

I bless thee.

With my waltzes.

It is strong!

Yet sweet.

With the quickest air following me.

O, sweet aroma.

Follow me everywhere around.

"In your fiery sun"

"In your twilight moon"

The Waltzing Stars

The twinkle of an eye.
On the stars, we glide.
Up there.
In the sky.
They dance and fly around.
We below watch in astonishment.
Fly around, stars.
Playing the tune in the skies above.
They fly with passion and dignity.
They chuckle.
They laugh.
All eyes can see.
What those stars were meant to be.
They fly.
They fly.
With dignity and courage!

Fly, my stars fly high!

Write to me from the Orion.

And fly high above those clouds.

Let your instruments play the most beautiful sounds.

Write to me from the Orion.

Once more, fly my stars.

Fly high.

As all eyes can see, in pure courage on high.

The Grave of Sixteen

O, why can you not see from the grave?
On this joyful sorrow day.
I have become one, and I will pray.
For the light.
For the dark.
It is in all tapestry.
That we will become one in humanity.
No more drought.
No more hope.
But with something that is in life.
Which forever copes.
Indeed, life is strange.
They will stand by my grave.
And the heaven's gate open.
And the hell's gate open.
On this joyful sorrow day.

There will always be light.
In the darkest night.
I wish on a star.
From how we can go so far.
O, this light.
Will forever bring me closer.
To this, I will hope more and more.
In my chambers, forever on, forever more.
O, how I see the candle lights dance away.
In all light, We walk with hope.
On this delightful day, I cope.
I wish to dance away.
The sorrows of my past days.
But, I will face them and lead them astray.
And hope on that bright star.
To which, I love,
Forever on,
Forever More.

All I see is black.
The abyss rising in stack.
The cold heart of this world.
Will kill me and O, how this world!
Will break and fall in the black abyss.
It will bring forever blackness, forever darkness.
O, I wish to fall and die!

www.ingramcontent.com/pod-product-compliance
Lightning Source LLC
LaVergne TN
LVHW021352080426
835508LV00020B/2237

THE GRAVE OF SIXTEEN

I wish to be rotten and die!
For it is all bones and decaying.
No more joy,
no more hope,
no more praying.
And I will weep and cry to forever die!
Inside my aching heart.
There is nothing like the start!
It will break my black cold heart!
And I will rest in the grave.
Nothing more but with hope around my bleeding sores.